flower of knowledge, good, and evil

Brianna Connelly

BookLeaf Publishing

India | USA | UK

Presentation by *BookLeaf Publishing*

Web: www.bookleafpub.com

E-mail: info@bookleafpub.com

ISBN: 9789357443487

First edition 2022

DEDICATION

*to the me who had not yet mistaken darkness for
light.*

ACKNOWLEDGEMENT

I had a few significant inspirations for these poems that deserve my gratitude. There are little components of both music and literature that make up the thematic elements of the book. Ritt Momney's music inspires my style of writing. I love the way specific words that symbolize his past are incorporated into his songs lyrics and titles. The authenticity within his work is like a masterclass in itself. Though he has no idea the impact he has had on me, I'd like to thank him. The main literarure references allude biblically to the "Garden of Eden," and mythologically to "The Rape of Proserpina." Though mythology and christianity appear to reside on opposite sides of ideological thinking, I find that Eve and Persephone are alarmingly similar when used symbolically. So symbolically, I chose to use them to illustrate my own circumstances.

PREFACE

I used to feel incapable of putting words to the intangible thoughts and feelings in my head. While I think I have gotten slightly better at painting a picture with words, I still marvel at the way authors and poets so indirectly convey meaning. I cannot claim that my leniency toward ambiguity is a product of mastering their skills, but really just a way for me to hide behind big words. If one does not understand what I write, the less I will have been revealed. Which introduces the underlying theme of the book.

There is a kind of rapid manifestation that comes with an obsession. An obsession with wanting to be smaller does not limit itself to physicality. Infact, it does not know when to stop pursuing itself. My initial longings to lose weight transformed into extreme psychological cravings to be viewed as small as possible. From there, I began to find more and more reasons to continue restrictive behavior, all which are of self depreciative nature. I have convinced myself that for whatever reason, I do not deserve luxuries like others do. Guilt, driven by the notion that I have not worked hard enough or am being self indulgent, overwhelms me the moment I feel a tinge of enjoyment. Point being, these disorders are so much more than calories in calories out. They are a complete brainwashing that results in physiological and mental withdrawal that can feel inescapable. As eating disorders are very complex, I feel that free verse poetry is the best outlet. I did my best in these poems to fully encapsulate what it is like to have these voices dominating your head. Of course, some poems stray from the prompt, but I'd like to think they all tie into the main idea since they all flowed from the same source. So here is, flower of knowledge, good, and evil.

*

this desire to leave no trace
woven through hidden outline
though this notion should not be displaced
to bring my knees to my chest with no barrier
is what i everyday shall face.
only now can i wither to nothing.

the forbidden fruit

I picked a flower I thought was lovely
but the sediment split at its roots
and the earth swallowed me whole
dirt filled my mouth and lungs
my mind and soul
and held me in the darkness.

trapped in black
I began to wonder
the validity of my state
for the light,
it never did me any good
it shone brightly against my face
spotlighting my flaws
deterring every means of comfort.

the earth in my chest
is cold,
but it warms me
enough to see the prayer
but hesitate upon the first word.

hooked up to the machine of earth,
I lie dormant and satisfied
with my new source of life
running from the roots
straight into my veins.

vines of old

I longed to be enough for someone
but I lost myself in the process.
I took too many turns and never left a trail,
now I am lost in a forest of uncertainty
surrounded by the mockery of endless shrubs.
They told me they would lead me to you
and now when I need you the most,
I don't even have myself.

box vs square

how bittersweet
to be one-dimensional
am I grateful because you can never be filled?
or do I envy that you will never be empty.

white flag

often I am surprised by the consistencies
of everything but this flesh.
the same voice that pushed me then
to be foreknowing and acknowledging
screams the same,
but holds a different demeanor.

and though I have carved out this truth
my eyes finally adjusted to the shadow,
it seems that it was made stronger by my
conscious
for what can I do but raise my white flags?
to fight would be to lose
compliance is strength in the eyes of the one
who speaks.

perceptions

victim, I am anything but
I was never a predator
save for myself
I seldom think upon the days we shared
physically cowering at the thought
of what I did to you
for the sake of my own vainness.

it was not the feeling of your lips on mine
it was the fear of my lips on yours
what might you feel in that moment
how will I be revealed?

but once we touch you will see,
and you will forever own a part of me
that should have remained hidden.

- the other side of heartbreak

control freak

"you look so much older!" they say with what
they think is delight
but they don't know
I can age backwards within days
if I just loosened the grip on the reigns.
but why would I
if they said it with delight.

the morning after

I wake still holding myself
tentative memories pulsing behind my eyes
its days like these I long to hide despite myself
days that I wish for the moon to rise
for the time I can release the small tether in my
head
and be.

lapsing

with each passing day
loveliness is undone

they don't see the cause
only the change

and turn their shoulders at the sight
of the girl getting better.

the trees listen

no breath is more alive
than the wood of the trees
keep conscious when you speak,
because the same bloodless oak
that ceases at the tip of a branch,
runs down under through the soil
all the way to the edges of the earth
whispering word of mouth.

silence.

eyes fluttering, shoulders slumped, lips parted,
shallow breaths, quiet mind.
when I follow the words of the voice,
it leaves me alone
and I can sit in peace
with an empty stomach
and an empty head.

screwtape

he is so much louder than all of you
everything is his area of expertise
and nothing is free of his knowledge.

lavender hand soap

remnants of lavender
stains these guilty fingers
while lovely in my nose,
purple stains my throat
inching up from my stomach
where the flower lies burned
in ashes of fulfilled fate.

repetitive mornings

do my bones know
that when I first open my eyes.
they are where my mind goes?
my hands rush to, seeking the sharp edges
and their absence
is enough to leave me
cowering in my skin
if I do better,
tomorrow we will encounter again.

tipping your scale

disturbed by crossed lines,
her father inquires very often
about the manner of his daughters dress.
she cannot take offense to his judgment
for his little girl reflects him too well.

what he should know
is that she takes comfort
in the heavy hug of big sweaters
smelling of old wooden drawers
and the distortion of her body
that comes with hiding away.

beyond reflections

mirror mirror on the wall
she who has it worst of all
i don't look sick
so surely im not
while she earns pity
i will have been forgot

hyper-everything

for your convenience
I will do so.
I will shut down the voice in my head
the voice that inflames at the drop of a pin
I will foreknow the words you speak
and shut out any noise that tries to enter
blood will not drip from your bitten tongue
today.
go ahead and speak mindlessly.

"mental toughness"

if i can go longer
why shouldn't i
because i was told to have discipline
not when.

elixir

It was the first time, since the last time you
touched me
unexpected as so
like electricity through your bones upon mine
you touched my negativity charged body
and with a painful shock the gaps filled
you understood where I have been.
but the current was strong enough
to break the ice over my chest
someone stopped over where I lay in the ground,
and reached out their hand.

A≠bxh

eyes that seek and chase
the circumstances that predispose storybooks
will all come to see one day
that their reign never came
the life they poured rivers of control
and constructed frameworks of dams
was never deigned to be
anything more than insatiably abstract.

minds that ponder and fabricate
the words that will be spoken
when their souls no longer reside
will all come to see one day
that the box in which they will eternally lie
holds the congruence and proportion
that only in the absence of life
they will finally accomplish.

*

22

since I was young
I imagined myself sprinting through the line in
the ground
but in real life, my toes only skim the edge
pushed back by the momentum of those
speeding past
I am unable to move from where I am
and watching their smiles from the other side
hurts more than the choke reality has on my
neck
for who am I to want to be in their place
who said I was worthy of glory
who said I was worthy of fulfillment.

in another world
I am running through the woods
over every stick in the dirt
leaving in the dust
every noose that tried to claim my life
overcoming every voice that ever said
I was never worthy of running
of succeeding
of loving.

but until my soul passes
I shall remain banished
locked out from that place in my head
always questioning what I did wrong
to deserve to be kept
on this side of reality.

9 789357 443487